STATES

MICHIGAN

A MyReportLinks.com Book

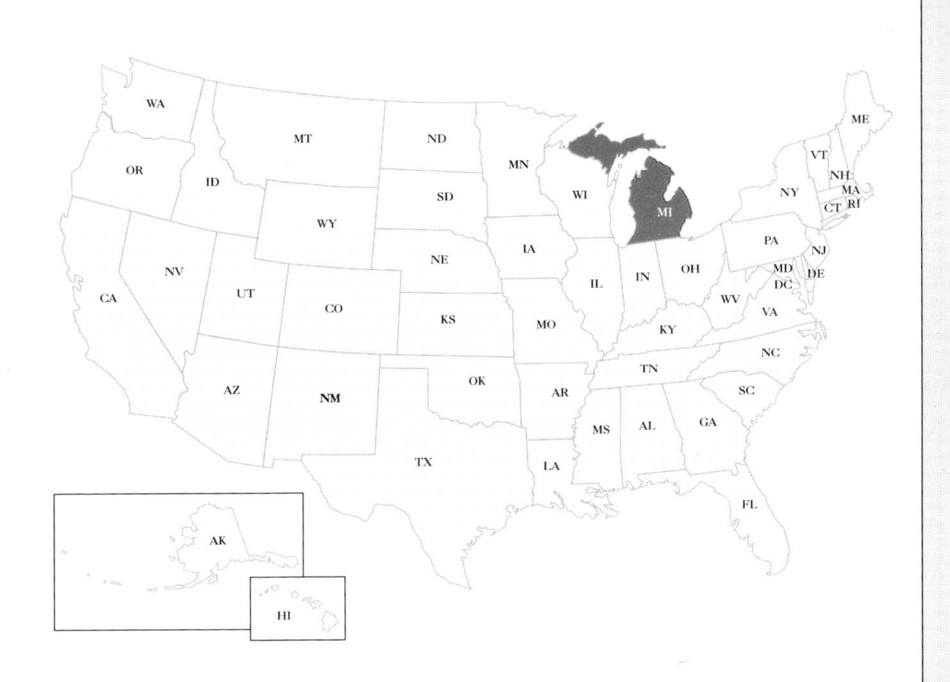

David Aretha

MyReportLinks.com Books

an imprint of

Enslow Publishers, Inc.

Box 398, 40 Industrial Road
Berkeley Heights, NJ 07922
USA

MyReportLinks.com Books, an imprint of Enslow Publishers, Inc. MyReportLinks is a trademark of Enslow Publishers, Inc.

Library of Congress Cataloging-in-Publication Data

Aretha, David.
Michigan / David Aretha.
p. cm. — (States)
Summary: Discusses the land and climate, economy, government, and history of the state of Michigan. Includes Internet links to Web sites.
Includes bibliographical references and index.
ISBN 0-7660-5154-4
1. Michigan—Juvenile literature. [1. Michigan.] I. Title. II. States (Series : Berkeley Heights, N.J.)
F566.3.A74 2003
977.4—dc21

2003009931

Printed in the United States of America

10 9 8 7 6 5 4 3 2 1

To Our Readers:
Through the purchase of this book, you and your library gain access to the Report Links that specifically back up this book.
The Publisher will provide access to the Report Links that back up this book and will keep these Report Links up to date on **www.myreportlinks.com** for three years from the book's first publication date.
We have done our best to make sure all Internet addresses in this book were active and appropriate when we went to press. However, the author and the Publisher have no control over, and assume no liability for, the material available on those Internet sites or on other Web sites they may link to.
The usage of the MyReportLinks.com Books Web site is subject to the terms and conditions stated on the Usage Policy Statement on **www.myreportlinks.com**.
A password may be required to access the Report Links that back up this book. The password is found on the bottom of page 4 of this book.
Any comments or suggestions can be sent by e-mail to comments@myreportlinks.com or to the address on the back cover.

Photo Credits: AP/Wide World Photos, pp. 15, 28; ArtToday.com, pp. 21, 36, 39, 41; © Corel Corporation, p. 3; © 1995 PhotoDisc, pp. 11, 44-45; © Robesus, p. 10 (flag); Daimler Chrysler/Walter P. Chrysler Museum, p. 23; *Detroit Free Press,* p. 33; *Detroit News Online,* p. 43; Enslow Publishers, Inc., pp. 1, 18; Eyewire/Getty Images, p. 30; Great Lakes Information Network, p. 19; Library of Congress, pp. 3 (Constitution), 13; Michigan Historical Society, Department of History, Arts, and Libraries, p. 24; MyReportLinks.com Books, p. 4; The State of Michigan, pp. 26, 32; *Time* Magazine Online, p. 16.

Cover Photo: © Corel Corporation

Cover Description: Detroit

Contents

MyReportLinks.com Books

Great Books, Great Links, Great for Research!

MyReportLinks.com Books present the information you need to learn about your report subject. In addition, they show you where to go on the Internet for more information. The pre-evaluated Report Links that back up this book are kept up to date on **www.myreportlinks.com**. With the purchase of a MyReportLinks.com Books title, you and your library gain access to the Report Links that specifically back up that book. The Report Links save hours of research time and link to dozens—even hundreds—of Web sites, source documents, and photos related to your report topic.

Please see "To Our Readers" on the Copyright page for important information about this book, the MyReportLinks.com Books Web site, and the Report Links that back up this book.

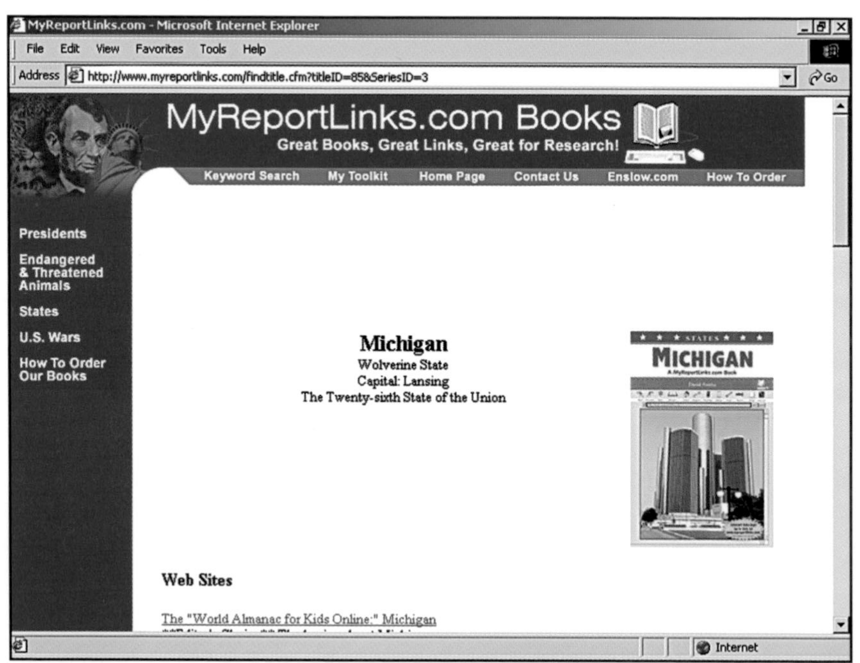

Access:

The Publisher will provide access to the Report Links that back up this book and will try to keep these Report Links up to date on our Web site for three years from the book's first publication date. Please enter **SMI2853** if asked for a password.

Report Links

The Internet sites described below can be accessed at **http://www.myreportlinks.com**

*Editor's Choice

▶The *World Almanac for Kids Online:* Michigan

This site contains an overview of vital Michigan state facts. Here you will find information about land and resources, population, education and cultural activity, government and politics, economy, and history.

Link to this Internet site from http://www.myreportlinks.com

*Editor's Choice

▶Explore the States: Michigan

This site from the Library of Congress tells the story of Michigan. You can learn the meaning of the name "Michigan" as well as read some interesting articles about the state.

Link to this Internet site from http://www.myreportlinks.com

*Editor's Choice

▶Henry Ford Museum & Greenfield Village

Visit the Henry Ford Museum & Greenfield Village, where the history of American invention and life is preserved for you to see. You can view an exhibit about the history of toys and so much more!

Link to this Internet site from http://www.myreportlinks.com

*Editor's Choice

▶U.S. Census Bureau: Michigan

This site from the United States Census Bureau contains facts and figures relating to the state of Michigan. Here you will find population, demographic, and housing information, economic statistics, and more.

Link to this Internet site from http://www.myreportlinks.com

*Editor's Choice

▶MI Kids!

This site from the state of Michigan provides information on historical events, tourist attractions, the government, and much more. Be sure to play the State Symbols Multiple Choice Game.

Link to this Internet site from http://www.myreportlinks.com

*Editor's Choice

▶Introduction to the Great Lakes

From the Education and Curriculum Homesite comes information on the Great Lakes. You can find out about each lake. Fun facts are also provided.

Link to this Internet site from http://www.myreportlinks.com

The Internet sites described below can be accessed at **http://www.myreportlinks.com**

▶BBCi: The 1936–37 Flint, Michigan Sit-Down Strike

The 1936–37 sit-down strike in Flint, Michigan, was one of the most notable clashes between management and workers in the history of the American labor movement. This BBC page tells the story—from the events leading up to the strike—to its legacy.

Link to this Internet site from http://www.myreportlinks.com

▶Coleman Alexander Young—1918–1997

Coleman Young was the first African-American mayor of Detroit and the city's longest-serving chief executive. This site explores his life and times. Here you will find an in-depth biography, a chronology of his life, his obituary, dozens of photographs, audio excerpts from his funeral, and more.

Link to this Internet site from http://www.myreportlinks.com

▶The Detroit Institute of the Arts

The Detroit Institute of the Arts is one of the most prestigious art museums in the United States. Here you will learn about the permanent collection and new exhibits. Virtual tours of some collections and a Flash section about Edgar Degas are included.

Link to this Internet site from http://www.myreportlinks.com

▶*Detroit News:* Rearview Mirror

The *Detroit News* created this site about the history of Detroit. Here you will find articles about business, industry, government, institutions, life in Michigan, events, people, sports, and more.

Link to this Internet site from http://www.myreportlinks.com

▶General Motors: GM History

Along with Ford and DaimlerChrysler, General Motors is one of the three biggest American auto manufacturers. Here you will find the history of the company and its cars.

Link to this Internet site from http://www.myreportlinks.com

▶George Armstrong Custer

General George Armstrong Custer distinguished himself in the Civil War and Indian Wars. He is most famous for his death and defeat at the Battle of the Little Bighorn. This page from the PBS series *New Perspectives on the West* contains his biography.

Link to this Internet site from http://www.myreportlinks.com

Report Links

The Internet sites described below can be accessed at **http://www.myreportlinks.com**

▶ Gerald Rudolph Ford (1974–1977)

At this Web site you will find a comprehensive biography of President Gerald R. Ford. Learn about his early life, domestic and foreign policies, the first lady, and much more.

Link to this Internet site from http://www.myreportlinks.com

▶ History Television: Siege of Detroit

The Siege of Detroit was the most elaborate uprising in American-Indian history. Here you will learn about the siege. Read articles about Pontiac, the Battle of Bloody Run, and significant moments in Ottawa history.

Link to this Internet site from http://www.myreportlinks.com

▶ Joe Louis: The Official Web Site

Joe Louis held the World Heavyweight Boxing Championship longer than any other man in history. Here at his official web site you will find his biography, photos, quotes, and career facts.

Link to this Internet site from http://www.myreportlinks.com

▶ Michigan Educational Portal for Interactive Content

The Michigan EPIC site contains interactive pages about the Flint Sit-Down Strike of 1936, Michigan governors, the United States' first female lighthouse keeper, and more. Audio, video, time lines, photographs, and other media tell the stories.

Link to this Internet site from http://www.myreportlinks.com

▶ Mining in Michigan

This site from the Michigan Historical Museum provides information on the mining industry in Michigan.

Link to this Internet site from http://www.myreportlinks.com

▶ NBA History: Magic Johnson

The Los Angeles Lakers' Magic Johnson is one of the best players in the history of the National Basketball Association. Here you will find his biography and career statistics.

Link to this Internet site from http://www.myreportlinks.com

Report Links

The Internet sites described below can be accessed at **http://www.myreportlinks.com**

▶ National Register of Historic Places: Detroit

This list from the National Register of Historic Places provides architectural and historic details of Detroit houses, neighborhoods, skyscrapers, churches, museums, and other places.

Link to this Internet site from http://www.myreportlinks.com

▶ Office of the Governor

At this site you can read a biography about Michigan's current governor, Jennifer M. Granholm. You will also find an archive of speeches and a listing of past governors.

Link to this Internet site from http://www.myreportlinks.com

▶ The Official Web Site of the Mackinac Bridge

The Mackinac Bridge is the longest suspension bridge in the Western Hemisphere. Here, at the official Web site of "Mighty Mac," you will find photographs, facts, history, web cams, news, and more.

Link to this Internet site from http://www.myreportlinks.com

▶ The Official State of Michigan Travel Web Site

Michigan.org is a guide to state tourism. Here you will find information about Michigan's museums, historic sites, state and national parks, zoos, lighthouses, events, and other attractions. Driving tours, interactive maps, and visitor information are included.

Link to this Internet site from http://www.myreportlinks.com

▶ The Official State of Michigan Web Site

Here at Michigan's official state site you will find a wide range of information pertaining to Michigan's government, history, arts, environment, geography, travel, and more.

Link to this Internet site from http://www.myreportlinks.com

▶ PBS: African American World—Malcolm X

This site from PBS provides a biography of Malcolm X, one of the most prominent figures in the history of the American civil rights movement. Follow the link at the bottom of the page to read his legendary "The Ballot or the Bullet" speech from 1964.

Link to this Internet site from http://www.myreportlinks.com

Report Links

The Internet sites described below can be accessed at
http://www.myreportlinks.com

▶ Rock and Roll Hall of Fame and Museum: Berry Gordy, Jr.
Berry Gordy, Jr., founded and managed one of the most important record labels in the history of popular music. This page from the Rock and Roll Hall of Fame and Museum contains a brief biography of this entrepreneur.

Link to this Internet site from http://www.myreportlinks.com

▶ Stately Knowledge: Michigan
Learn the facts about the state of Michigan. Read the state motto, and learn about Michigan's major industries and bordering states.

Link to this Internet site from http://www.myreportlinks.com

▶ Stuff About Michigan
Stuff About Michigan, from the Office of the Secretary of State, contains a wealth of state information. Here you will find important events in Michigan history, a list of famous state residents, an auto tour, symbols, and much more.

Link to this Internet site from http://www.myreportlinks.com

▶ *Time* 100: The Soul Musician—Aretha Franklin
Aretha Franklin is commonly recognized as the Queen of Soul music. Here you will find her biography from *Time* magazine's ranking of the one-hundred most influential artists and entertainers of the twentieth century.

Link to this Internet site from http://www.myreportlinks.com

▶ Vernor's History
Have you ever tasted Vernor's Ginger Ale? At this site you can read about America's oldest soda pop and how James Vernor created this popular brand.

Link to this Internet site from http://www.myreportlinks.com

▶ Walter P. Chrysler Museum
The Chrysler Museum is dedicated to the company's cars and the people who created them. Here you will find Chrysler history, biographical information about Walter P. Chrysler, an online tour of the museum, visitor information, and more.

Link to this Internet site from http://www.myreportlinks.com

Michigan Facts

Capital
Lansing

Gained Statehood
January 26, 1837

Counties
83

Population
9,938,444*

Bird
Robin

Tree
White pine

Flower
Apple blossom

Game Mammal
White-tailed deer

Reptile
Painted turtle

Fish
Brook trout

Gemstone
Isle Royal Greenstone

**Population reflects the 2000 census.*

Stone
Petoskey

Song
"Michigan, My Michigan" (written by William Otto Miessner and Douglas M. Malloch)

Motto
If you seek a pleasant peninsula, look about you.

Nicknames
Great Lakes State,
Wolverine State

Flag
Michigan's state coat of arms appears on a dark blue background. The coat of arms includes three phrases, all in Latin: *Si quaeris peninsulam amoenam, circumspice,* the state motto; *Tuebor,* which translates to "I will defend;" and *E pluribus unum,* the motto of the United States, which means "From many, one."

Chapter 1 ▶

The Great Lakes State

Ask Michiganders where they live and they will likely point to a spot on their right hand. That is because Michigan's Lower Peninsula is shaped like a mitten—one of several unique characteristics of the Great Lakes State.

Water Wonderland

Michigan is the only state comprised of two large land masses, the Lower Peninsula (L.P.) and Upper Peninsula (U.P). The two are connected by the majestic Mackinac Bridge. Otherwise, each peninsula is surrounded on three

Michigan is known as the Great Lakes State and is also called a Water Wonderland. The vast Lake Michigan is one reason why.

sides by water. Michigan features 3,288 miles of coastline. In Michigan, water is everywhere. The state contains about eleven thousand lakes and is nicknamed Water Wonderland. Not one of Michigan's 9.9 million residents is ever more than six miles from a lake.

Michigan's water has dazzled inhabitants for hundreds of years. The name of the state, Michigan, comes from the Chippewa words *michi-gama*, meaning "great water."

Europeans discovered Michigan's splendors by accident. French explorers sailed from New France (present-day Canada) in search of a passageway to Asia. Instead, they discovered the Upper Peninsula. The French explored the territory further, hoping to make money from selling pelts of the area's many fur-bearing animals. They hunted for fur and traded with American Indians for the valuable pelts. In the 1700s, the British tried to capitalize on the fur-trading business. They defeated the French and American Indians in the French and Indian War, and by 1763 the British ruled the territory.

In 1805, twenty-two years after the Revolutionary War ended, the Michigan Territory was recognized by the United States. Easterners considered Michigan a valuable resource for iron ore, lumber, and food crops. With the opening of the Erie Canal in 1825, thousands of Easterners flocked to Michigan to work the land. Many were awed by the beauty of the lakes. One visitor claimed that "as far as the eye can reach presents the most exquisite tints of the emerald, sparkling and leaping in the glad sunshine."[1]

Business in Michigan boomed in the late 1800s. Loggers cut billions of feet of pine logs per year. Michigan led the country in production of railroad cars and stoves. When Henry Ford of Detroit produced an affordable automobile during the early years of the twentieth century, a new industry was born.

Motor City

Each day, millions of Americans eat breakfast and then drive to work. They have Michiganders to thank for starting their day the way they are used to. Michigan supplies the world with cereal, fruit, dairy products, and—most notably—automobiles.

For a full century, Detroit has been the "Motor City." Auto giants Ford, General Motors, and DaimlerChrysler are all either based in or have large plants near Detroit.

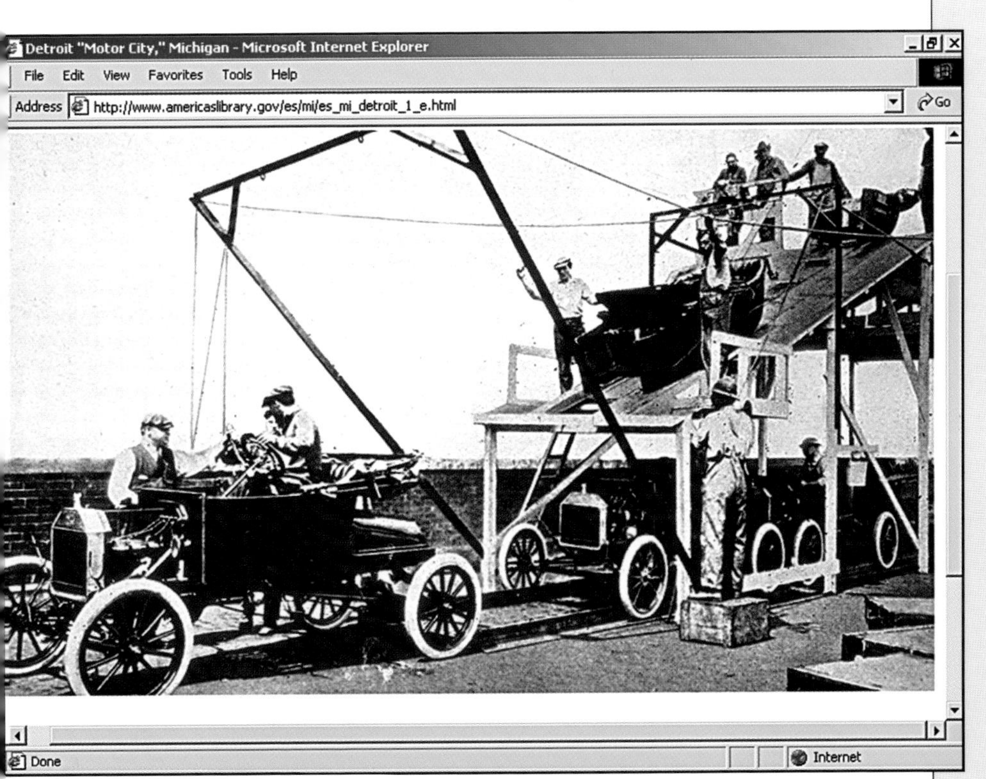

Detroit is nicknamed Motor City because it is recognized for being the base of the American auto industry. Henry Ford's automobile factory was the first to use a moving assembly line.

The Detroit metropolitan area (including outlying cities Ann Arbor and Flint) is home to 5.5 million people. Many of them work in or contribute to the auto industry.

Detroit's love affair with cars is unmistakable. The Henry Ford Museum in Detroit attracts hundreds of thousands of visitors each year. In suburban Romulus, an eighty-foot-high Uniroyal tire looms over I-94. Ford Motor Company features a tote board that flashes the number of cars that roll off its assembly lines. In 2000, that number exceeded four million.

Many Resources

Battle Creek, the "Cereal Bowl of America," lies 120 miles west of the Motor City. Each day, Kellogg's, located in Battle Creek, produces several million boxes of cereal. The state is also one of the country's top milk producers. To round out the breakfast, Michigan produces more blueberries than any other state. For lunch, the hot dog—loaded with chili—is a Detroit delicacy. Locals enjoy their franks with the nose-tingling Vernor's Ginger Ale, America's oldest soda pop, originally produced and sold in Detroit.

City dwellers looking for fun zoom north on I-75. Northern Michigan is a recreational playground that hosts several million vacationers each year. Tourists may fish, hike, hunt, sail, ski, and play golf. Such tourist havens as Traverse City and Charlevoix lure visitors with their beauty and charm. Others take a ferry to Mackinac Island, home of world-famous Mackinac Island Fudge. Real adventurers travel to the Upper Peninsula, which features majestic mountains and steep waterfalls.

Michigan's Rock 'n' Soul

Thanks to Berry Gordy, Jr., Detroit will forever be known as "Motown." Gordy, a Ford factory worker, borrowed $800 in

Berry Gordy, Jr., founded Motown Records in Detroit in 1959.

1959 and founded Motown Records. "I wanted a place where a kid off the street could walk in one door an unknown and come out another a recording artist—a star," he said.[2] Gordy attracted the best African-American singers and musicians, including many from Michigan. Stevie Wonder, from Saginaw, became a Motown superstar by age twelve in 1963. Diana Ross and the Supremes (Mary Wilson and Florence Ballard), all from Detroit, recorded five straight No. 1 hits in 1964. Aretha Franklin, singing "R-E-S-P-E-C-T," became the Queen of Soul. In the 1960s, Motown was perhaps America's most popular music.

As the nation's eighth largest state, Michigan has been home to some of the most important people in American history. Henry Ford was an auto industry pioneer who helped perfect the factory assembly line. Charles Lindbergh captivated the world in 1927, becoming the first to fly a plane solo across the Atlantic Ocean. In 1938, boxing champion Joe Louis, who was born in Alabama but lived moved to Detroit, became a national hero. The "Brown Bomber," as he was known, was heavyweight champion for twelve years.

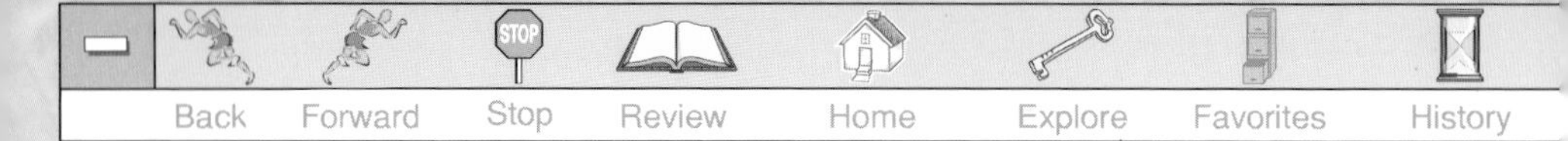

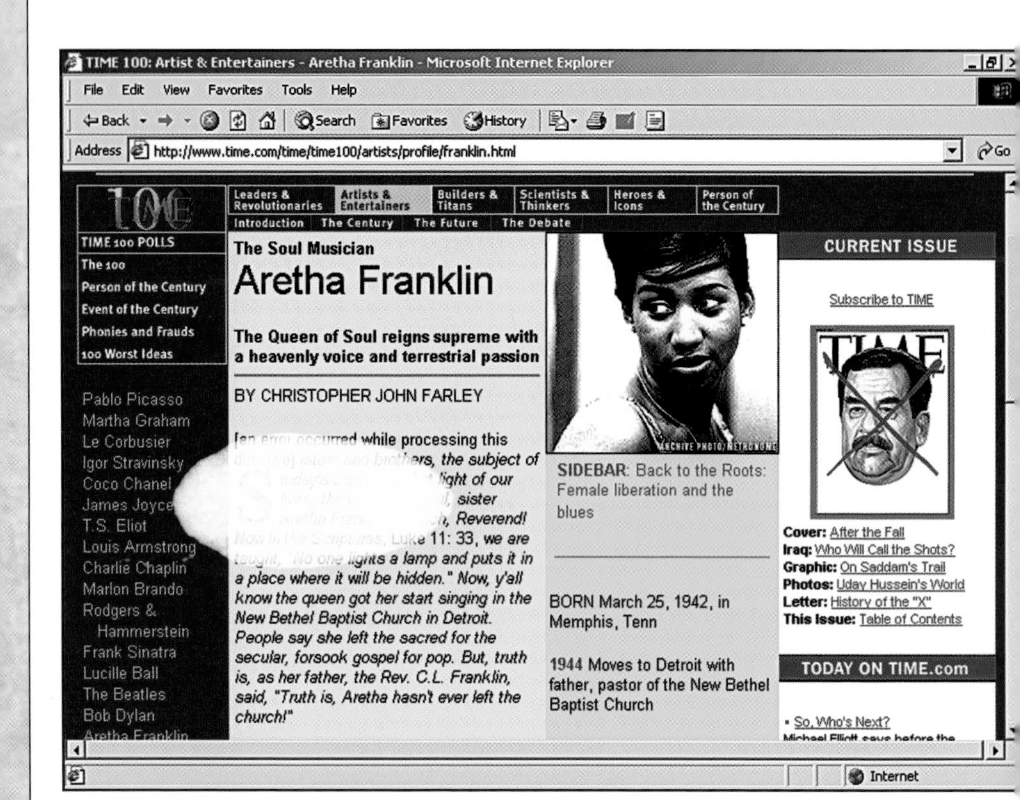

TIME 100: Artist & Entertainers - Aretha Franklin - Microsoft Internet Explorer
File Edit View Favorites Tools Help
Back Search Favorites History
Address http://www.time.com/time/time100/artists/profile/franklin.html
Go
Leaders & Revolutionaries
Artists & Entertainers
Builders & Titans
Scientists & Thinkers
Heroes & Icons
Person of the Century
Introduction The Century The Future The Debate
TIME 100 POLLS
The 100
Person of the Century
Event of the Century
Phonies and Frauds
100 Worst Ideas
Pablo Picasso
Martha Graham
Le Corbusier
Igor Stravinsky
Coco Chanel
James Joyce
T.S. Eliot
Louis Armstrong
Charlie Chaplin
Marlon Brando
Rodgers & Hammerstein
Frank Sinatra
Lucille Ball
The Beatles
Bob Dylan
The Soul Musician
Aretha Franklin
The Queen of Soul reigns supreme with a heavenly voice and terrestrial passion
BY CHRISTOPHER JOHN FARLEY
a place where it will be hidden." Now, y'all know the queen got her start singing in the New Bethel Baptist Church in Detroit. People say she left the sacred for the secular, forsook gospel for pop. But, truth is, as her father, the Rev. C.L. Franklin, said, "Truth is, Aretha hasn't ever left the church!"
SIDEBAR: Back to the Roots: Female liberation and the blues
BORN March 25, 1942, in Memphis, Tenn
1944 Moves to Detroit with father, pastor of the New Bethel Baptist Church
CURRENT ISSUE
Subscribe to TIME
TIME
Cover: After the Fall
Iraq: Who Will Call the Shots?
Graphic: On Saddam's Trail
Photos: Uday Hussein's World
Letter: History of the "X"
This Issue: Table of Contents
TODAY ON TIME.com
So, Who's Next?
Internet

Aretha Franklin is known as the Queen of Soul. She was born to gospel-singing parents and joined the church choir at the age of twelve. She won a Grammy for performing the song "Respect" and was the first woman inducted into the Rock and Roll Hall of Fame.

In the 1980s, Earvin "Magic" Johnson revitalized the National Basketball Association with his amazing talent and million-dollar smile. The 1980s also belonged to a pop superstar from Rochester, Michigan. Madonna's *Like a Virgin* album from 1984 sold 10 million copies, and she greatly influenced the fashion world. The list of Michigan heroes and popular figures, like the vastness of its lakes, seems to go on forever.

Chapter 2 ▶

Land and Climate

Michigan is the largest of the twenty-six states located east of the Mississippi River. The Upper and Lower Peninsulas (U.P. and L.P.) comprise 96,810 square miles. The U.P. borders not the L.P. but Wisconsin. The Lower Peninsula is surrounded by the Great Lakes on the east, north, and west. Michigan "sits atop" Ohio and Indiana.

About two million years ago, glaciers (large masses of ice) moved south across Canada and the United States. Their effect on Michigan was spectacular. The glaciers dug five extra-large basins in the land, which became the Great Lakes. They also created thousands of other lakes, mountains, hills, valleys, rivers, and waterfalls.

Geologists divide Michigan's land into two parts: Superior Upland and Central Lowland. The Superior Upland, which includes the western half of the U.P., is rugged territory. It features the Huron and Porcupine mountain ranges, which attracts the Midwest's bravest skiers. The peak of Huron's Mount Arvon is 1,979 feet high, making it Michigan's tallest mountain. The region contains enormous deposits of copper and iron ore. Pine forests, dairy farms, and sparkling lakes make for a glorious drive.

The Lower Peninsula and the eastern half of the U.P. comprise the Central Lowland. Though relatively flat, the region includes many special features. The Sleeping Bear Dunes National Lakeshore along Lake Michigan includes sand dunes that rise 400 feet. The upper half of the L.P. is forested. Oak, maple, hickory, and elm trees—as well as

A map of Michigan.

cherry and apple trees—shade the land. Hundreds of thousands of deer enjoy the solitude . . . at least until hunting season. Much of the L.P. brims with rich soil. Tens of thousands of farmers take advantage of the land.

Glaciers created natural wonders in the eastern U.P. Frigid rivers, highlighted by scores of waterfalls, flow through hills and valleys. Isle Royale, located far above the U.P. in Lake Superior, is a national park. Moose and wolves await the rare visitors.

Great Lakes

Michiganders will never be thirsty. After all, the five Great Lakes contain six quadrillion gallons of water. That is 600 million gallons for each of Michigan's 9.9 million residents! The Great Lakes contain 95 percent of North America's fresh surface water.

At 31,700 square miles, Lake Superior is the largest freshwater lake in the world. It is so huge that it can hold

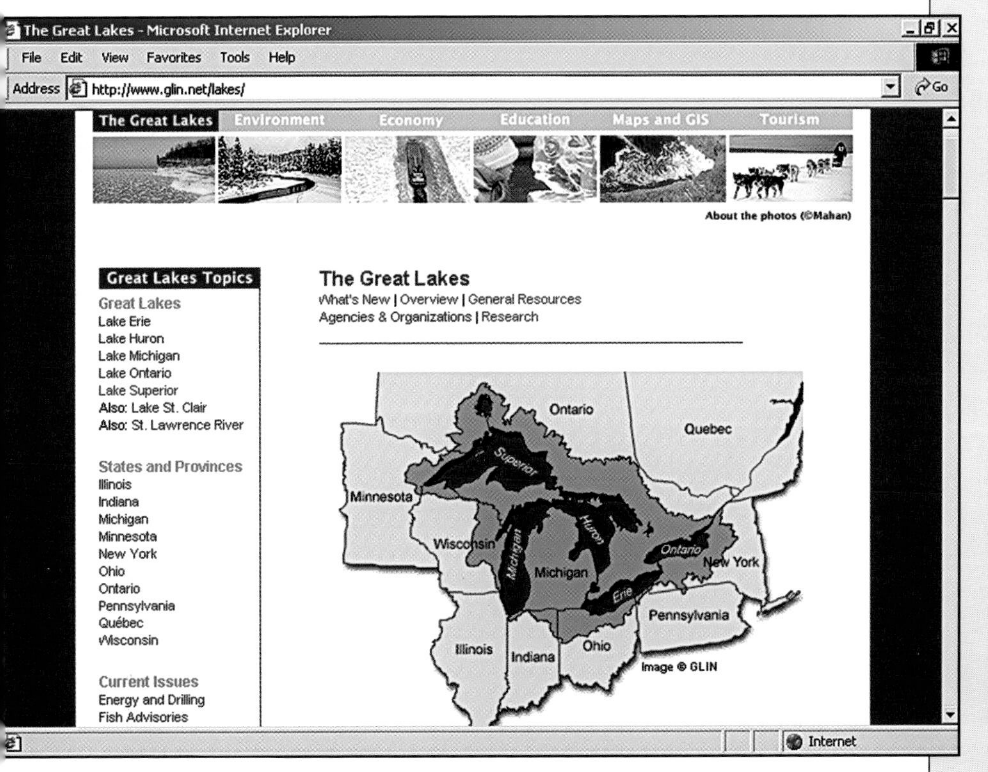

The Great Lakes and their channels form the largest freshwater surface on earth and can be seen from the moon. The Lakes' water would be 9.5 feet deep if spread evenly across the contiguous forty-eight states.

the combined water of the other four Great Lakes. Bordering the Upper Peninsula and Canada, Superior's water is perpetually cold. Numerous ships have plunged to its bottom, which drops to a low point of 1,332 feet below the surface. The *Edmund Fitzgerald,* popularized in a song by Gordon Lightfoot, disappeared into Lake Superior in November 1975.

Lake Michigan separates Michigan from Wisconsin and Illinois. It, too, is enormous—the fourth largest freshwater lake on earth. Lake Michigan flows through the Straits of Mackinac, located at the "top" of the Lower Peninsula, and into Lake Huron. Huron is slightly larger than Lake Michigan. It borders Michigan's "thumb" area and Ontario, Canada. Incredibly, Lake Huron engulfs approximately thirty thousand islands. Lake Erie borders Michigan, Ontario, Ohio, Pennsylvania, and New York. Lake Erie and Lake Ontario are among the world's twelve largest lakes. Ontario is the only one of the Great Lakes not adjacent to Michigan.

Cannot Wait Till Summer

Summers in Michigan can be wonderfully mild. From June through September, temperatures usually hover in the 70s and 80s in the Lower Peninsula. The southern L.P. experiences a few days in the 90s, and the humidity can be high during July and August. On July 13, 1936, the temperature in Mio, Michigan, soared to 113 degrees—the highest ever recorded in the state.

In Michigan, autumn runs from late September into November (although it can start earlier in the U.P.). October is spectacular, as the greenery explodes into orange, yellow, and red. In late November, however, residents prepare for a long, cold, overcast winter. Because of

Built in 1874, the Little Sable Lighthouse continues to guide ships sailing on Lake Michigan.

the moisture above the Great Lakes, Michigan is one of the cloudiest states in the country. During the coldest month, January, the average highs range from the low 30s (southern L.P.) to about 20 degrees (northern U.P.). On February 9, 1934, the temperature in Vanderbilt, Michigan, plummeted to 51 degrees below zero.

Snowfall varies more dramatically. Detroit typically gets 30 to 40 inches of snow per year, while the upper U.P. can be deluged with 30 feet of snow! April highs in Detroit can range from the 30s to the 80s, teasing and frustrating residents.

Chapter 3

Economy

From the copper miners of Houghton to the factory workers of Detroit, Michiganders are known for their work ethic. One worker, Fabian Fournier of Saginaw, was one such lumberjack that some claim inspired the legend of Paul Bunyan.

Most people in the state work in the service industry. Michiganders are doctors, bankers, insurance agents, government workers, drycleaners, and so on. However, Michigan still ranks among the nation's leaders in producing goods. Two of its top industries are manufacturing and agriculture. Tourism also ranks as a multibillion-dollar industry.

Made in Michigan

Tens of millions of the cars and trucks on the road were manufactured by Detroit's automakers: Ford, General Motors, and DaimlerChrysler. Yet Michigan's auto industry goes far beyond the Big Three. Numerous companies provide the auto giants with parts, such as fenders, mirrors, and tires. More than 80 percent of America's automobile research-and-development facilities are located in Michigan. Factories and shops manufacture drills, springs, wires, and dies (cutting and shaping tools).

People in northern Michigan work the land. Miners in Michigan and Minnesota supply more than 80 percent of the country's iron ore, which is shipped to steel companies. Men and women work the earth for oil, natural gas, and limestone. In Michigan, the timber industry generates close to $2 billion a year for the state economy. Michigan

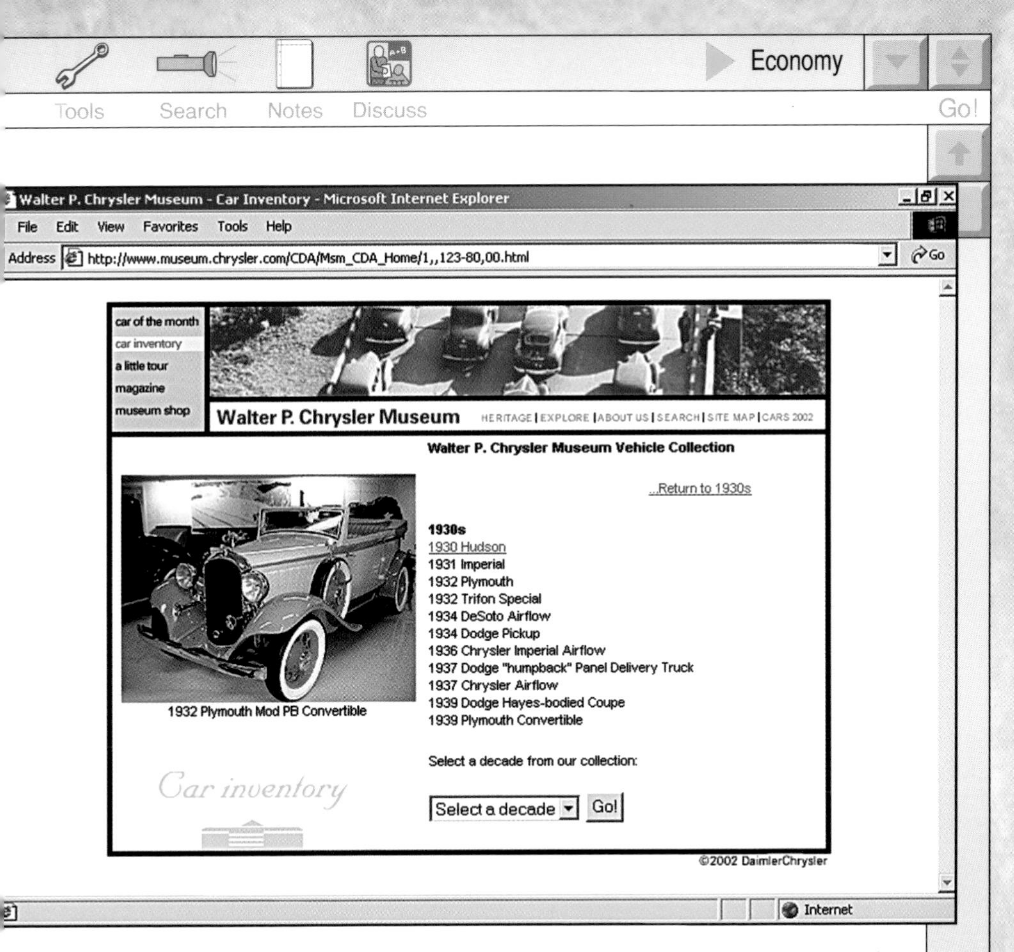

Chrysler, one of the leading car manufacturers in the country, was founded in Auburn Hills, Michigan. The Walter P. Chrysler Museum opened in 1999.

boasts the largest variety of commercial tree species, including pine and hickory. Each December, four million Michigan-grown Christmas trees are lit and decorated.

Historically, car making, mining, and lumbering have been Michigan's big industries, but the state has become much more diversified. Companies produce electronic appliances, from refrigerators to computers. Grand Rapids, Michigan's second largest city, specializes in furniture. Dow Chemical and Upjohn reign as giants in the chemical industry. Gerber has been making baby food since 1927. Kmart is headquartered in Southeast Michigan, as are pizza

Back
Forward
Stop
Review
Home
Explore
Favorites
History
Mining in Michigan Gallery, Michigan Historical Museum - Microsoft Internet Explorer
File Edit View Favorites Tools Help
Address http://www.sos.state.mi.us/history/museum/explore/museums/hismus/prehist/mining/index.html
Go
Mining in Michigan
Michigan Historical Museum
MINING IN MICHIGAN
A towering mine headframe of timber and a massive piece of float copper mark the entrance to the Mining in Michigan Gallery. Beyond are exhibits about copper and iron mining, life in Michigan's Upper Peninsula mining communities and the state's other mineral resources.
Tour the gallery:
Copper Mining
Iron Mining
Upper Peninsula Mining Communities
Salt to Coal
Shipping the Ore
Internet

At the Michigan Historical Museum you can learn about the history of mining. The Mining in Michigan Gallery has many exhibits of how copper, iron, and salt have been mined in the state.

makers Domino's and Little Caesars. In Battle Creek, Kellogg's does about $7 billion in business annually, feeding families in more than 150 countries.

Diversification has saved Michigan's economy. In the 1960s, and again in the 1980s, unemployment rates soared when the auto industry slumped. At the beginning of the twenty-first century, the state's economy was far less reliant on car making, and the unemployment rate in 2002 was below the national average. When Michigan's population jumped 6.9 percent from 1990 to 2000, analysts attributed the healthy increase to the state's strong economy.

A Bountiful Harvest

In the 1800s, lumber companies harvested thousands of acres of forest. Farmers moved in and took advantage of empty, fertile land. They prospered, too. Historian Bruce Catton wrote, "Michigan . . . is a state that grew up believing that abundance is forever."[1]

In 2002, Michigan boasted more than fifty thousand farms, and agriculture generated $37 billion for the state's economy. Michigan farmers grow more black beans, cranberry beans, cucumbers, blueberries, and tart cherries than any state in the country. Traverse City proudly calls itself America's Cherry Capital.

Michigan farmers raise dairy cattle, beef cattle, hogs, chickens, and turkeys. In 2001, Michigan dairy cattle produced 5.7 billion pounds of milk. Farmers also grow wheat, corn, soybeans, potatoes, and numerous other crops. Workers in the western L.P. help Midwesterners adorn their homes—Kalamazoo specializes in flowering and bedding plants, while the city of Holland brims with tulips.

Driving to Paradise

By producing so many cars and trucks, Michiganders indirectly created two new industries for the state—road construction and tourism. Auto sales boomed after World War II. Seemingly everybody had a car—and an urge to explore the open road. In the 1950s and beyond, Michigan's construction workers crisscrossed the state with highways. For Detroiters, the state's abundant treasures were just a car ride away.

Millions of people tour Michigan each year. Many tug their boats to the nearest big lake. Lake Michigan hosts the annual Chicago to Mackinac yacht race—an international

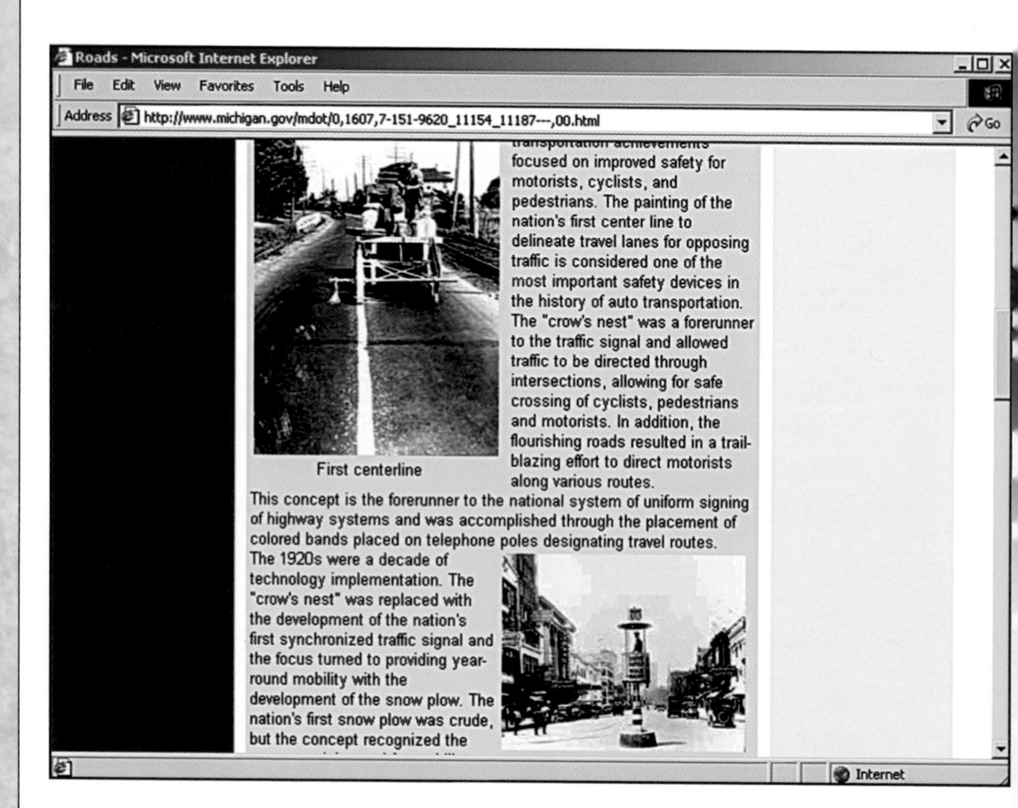
Roads - Microsoft Internet Explorer
File Edit View Favorites Tools Help
Address http://www.michigan.gov/mdot/0,1607,7-151-9620_11154_11187---,00.html

focused on improved safety for motorists, cyclists, and pedestrians. The painting of the nation's first center line to delineate travel lanes for opposing traffic is considered one of the most important safety devices in the history of auto transportation. The "crow's nest" was a forerunner to the traffic signal and allowed traffic to be directed through intersections, allowing for safe crossing of cyclists, pedestrians and motorists. In addition, the flourishing roads resulted in a trail-blazing effort to direct motorists along various routes. This concept is the forerunner to the national system of uniform signing of highway systems and was accomplished through the placement of colored bands placed on telephone poles designating travel routes.

First centerline

The 1920s were a decade of technology implementation. The "crow's nest" was replaced with the development of the nation's first synchronized traffic signal and the focus turned to providing year-round mobility with the development of the snow plow. The nation's first snow plow was crude, but the concept recognized the

Internet

Aside from being at the forefront of automobile manufacturing, Michigan also developed some of the first traffic regulations. The painting of the first center line and the building of the first traffic control tower occurred in Michigan.

event. The state's lakes and rivers brim with such fish as trout, perch, and bass.

Fall is "deer-hunting season" for many adventurers. Michigan ranks first among states in number of permissible deer-hunting days. For those who prefer to shoot low scores, Michigan boasts more than eight hundred public golf courses, the most in the country. Throughout the state, people are just minutes away from a hiking trail, bike path, or sandy beach. Come winter, skiers take advantage of Michigan's huge hills—and mountains in the northern reaches.

Sightseers enjoy visiting the quaint northern towns of Petosky, Harbor Springs, and Charlevoix. A ferry transports a million tourists per year to Mackinac Island—home of the fabled Grand Hotel. Many who venture to the U.P. flock to Tahquamenon Falls. Two hundred feet wide with a fifty-foot-drop, Tahquamenon is the second largest falls located east of the Mississippi River. At times, fifty thousand gallons of water per second cascade over its edge.

Detroit

Though not known as a tourist hot spot, Detroit features many unique attractions. The Henry Ford Museum revs up the interest of antique car buffs. Greenfield Village brings American history to life. Visitors, for example, can enter "Thomas Edison's laboratory." Detroit boasts one of America's largest zoos. In the summer, the outdoor Eastern Market captures the beat of the city: "heckling vendors, booming truck horns and wailing blues guys who sing and strum for pocket change."[2]

In the 1970s, the Renaissance Center was constructed to rejuvenate Detroit's downtown area. The "RenCen" rises seventy-three stories high and includes a hotel and shopping center. Minutes away is the world-famous Detroit Institute of Arts, which includes works by Vincent van Gogh, Edgar Degas, and Diego Rivera.

Detroiters love their sports teams. Baseball's Tigers and football's Lions each play in spectacular stadiums—Comerica Park and Ford Field. The Pistons won the National Basketball Association title in 1989 and 1990, while the Red Wings have turned Detroit into "Hockeytown." The Wings won the Stanley Cup in 1997,

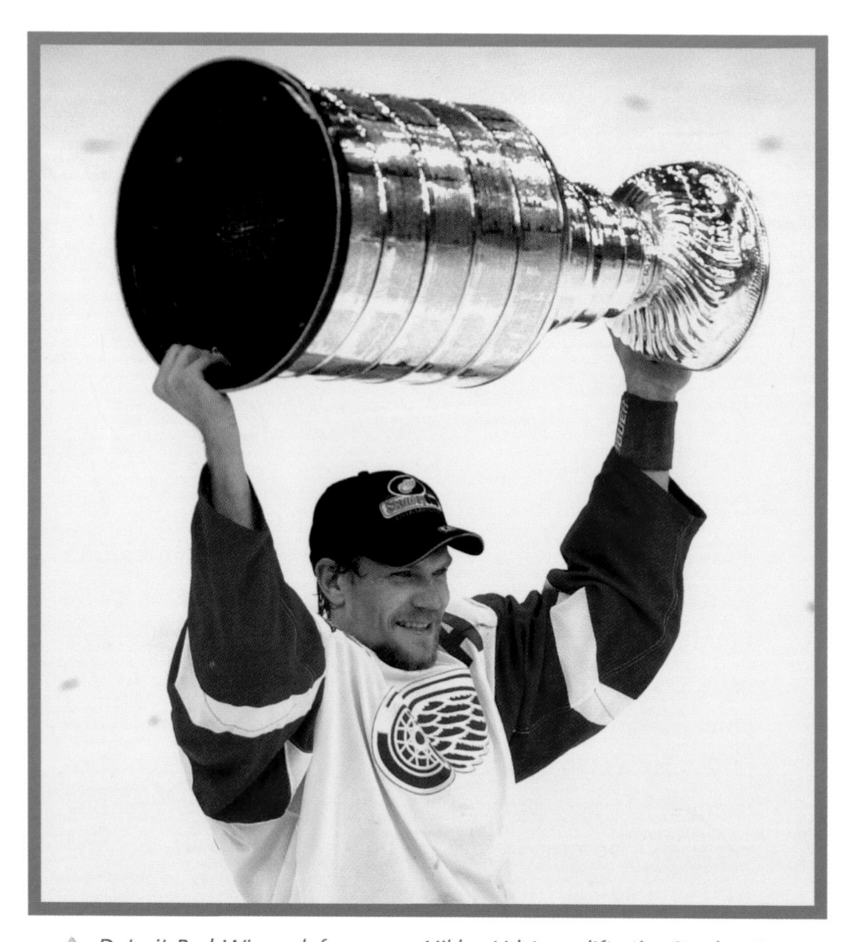

Detroit Red Wings defenseman Niklas Lidstrom lifts the Stanley Cup over his head, after his team wins the 2002 NHL championship. Professional sports help boost Michigan's economy.

1998, and 2002. Michiganders are fanatical about college football. Michigan State University draws more than 70,000 patrons per game, while the University of Michigan has attracted at least 100,000 fans to every contest since 1975. That is definitely one way to boost the economy!

Chapter 4 ▶

Government

The formative years of Michigan's government seem too outrageous to be believed. In 1805, General William Hull became the first governor of the Territory of Michigan. Yet when he arrived in Detroit, the new capital, he found the settlement burned to the ground.

In 1831, Stevens T. Mason, age nineteen, was appointed acting territorial secretary of Michigan Territory. When Governor George Porter died in 1834, Mason became governor—at age twenty-two! Thirteen years later, Michigan's legislators needed to name a new permanent capital. When someone suggested an area in Ingham County—home to just a few cabins—people laughed. Still, the legislators liked the area's central location. The site was named Lansing, which remains the state's capital.

The Structure of Michigan's Government

Michigan's constitution and government structure resemble those of the federal government. The state's constitution was written in 1835 and has been revised three times, most recently in 1964. The government is divided into three branches: legislative, executive, and judicial. The legislative branch creates the laws, the executive branch carries out and enforces state laws, and the judicial branch interprets the laws.

Michigan's governor is the state's chief executive. He or she supervises three elected officials: the lieutenant

When General William Hull became governor of the Michigan Territory he found that the former capital of Michigan had been burned to the ground. Detroit is no longer the capital, but remains the largest city in the state.

governor, attorney general, and the secretary of state. The governor also oversees state agencies such as the Treasury, Department of Agriculture, and Department of Education. The governor also serves as the spokesperson for Michigan, often trying to lure business to the state. The governor is elected to four-year terms.

Like the federal government, Michigan's legislative branch includes a senate (upper house) and a house of representatives (lower house). Senators and representatives propose new laws that they believe would best serve the state's citizens. If both houses pass a proposal (a bill), it is sent to the governor to sign into law. The governor can veto a bill, but the house and senate can vote to override the veto. Michigan's senate includes thirty-eight members, who are elected to four-year terms. The house has 110 members, elected to two-year terms.

In Michigan's judicial system, district courts deal with civil cases involving less than $25,000. Circuit courts hear larger civil cases as well as criminal cases. Those who lose in these lower courts can try to plead their case at the Michigan Court of Appeals. Some cases are appealed to the Michigan Supreme Court, which has the final decision. The supreme court includes seven justices, who are elected to eight-year terms.

A system of taxation funds the state government. Michigan citizens pay a state income tax, meaning that a small portion of their paychecks goes to the state government. They also pay a state sales tax, which is 6 percent. That means if someone buys a product in Michigan for $100, he or she will have to pay an additional $6 to the state. However, Michigan residents do not have to pay a local sales tax. The 6 percent overall sales tax is below the national average.

Lansing became the capital of Michigan in 1847. All state government offices can be found in the city.

Political Clashes

In Michigan, Republicans and Democrats often have butted heads. In presidential elections, candidates battle hard to win the Michigan vote—which can often go either way.

Early in the 1990s, Republican Governor John Engler caused a storm of controversy when he successfully pushed for tax cuts while slashing social programs. His plan helped spur Michigan's economy, but many less-fortunate citizens paid the price. Supporters of Engler say his "tough cuts" helped everyone in the long run.

Michigan's unemployment numbers and poverty rates have dropped dramatically.

Politicians

When United States Vice President Spiro Agnew resigned in 1973, President Richard Nixon picked Michigan Congressman Gerald Ford as the new vice president. Ford, from Grand Rapids, was a former football lineman and team MVP at the University of Michigan. When Nixon himself resigned in 1974, Ford became the thirty-eighth president of the United States. Historians credit

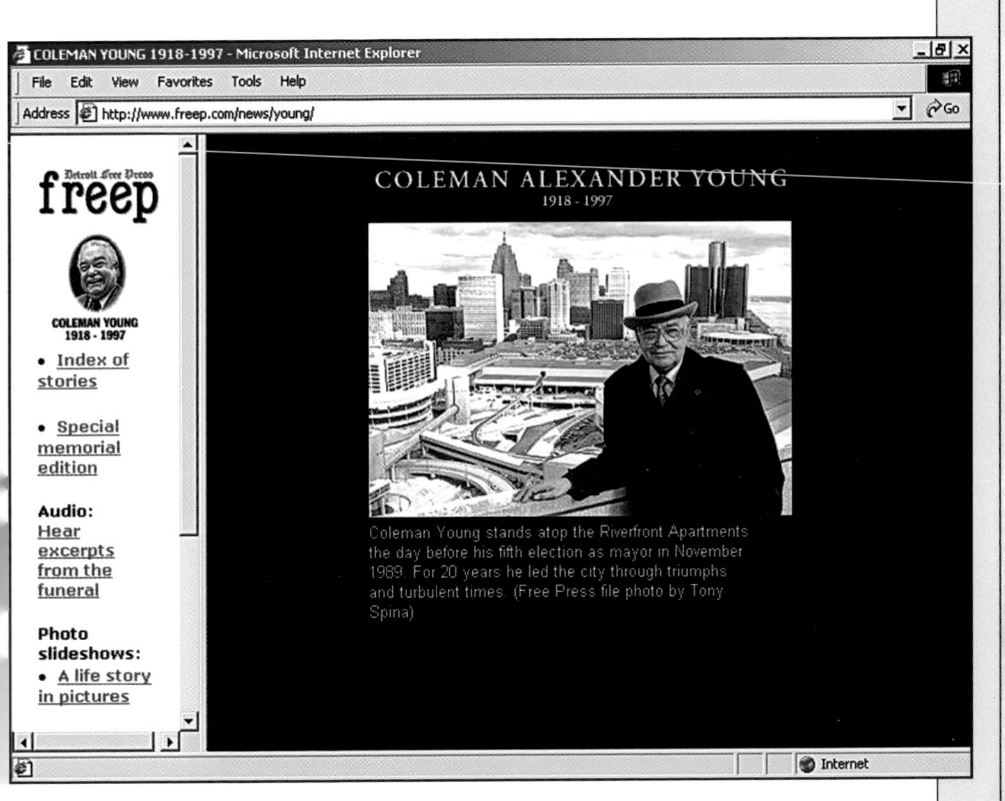

Coleman Alexander Young was born in Alabama in 1918 and moved to Detroit with his family in 1923. He was elected delegate to the Michigan Constitutional Convention in 1961 and was elected mayor of Detroit in 1973.

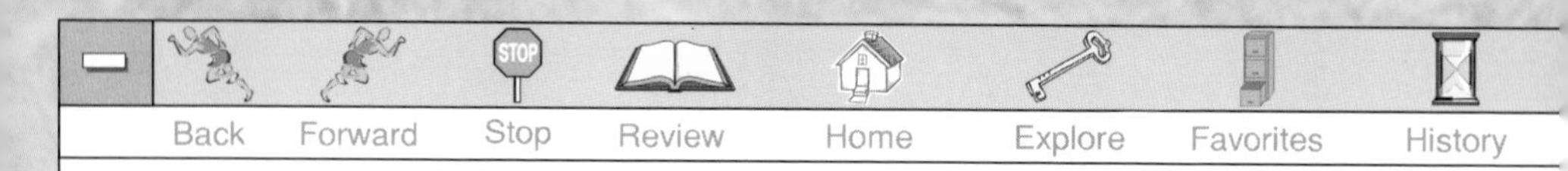

Ford with bringing honor and stability back to the White House.

Also in 1974, Coleman Young began his twenty-year tenure as Detroit's mayor. A prominent civil rights activist, Young helped create greater opportunities for Detroit's large African-American population. He worked to get more African Americans on the police force and in government positions. He also pushed for affordable housing and revitalized neighborhoods.

Ralph Bunche and Malcolm X are two other African Americans from Michigan who rose to prominence. Working for the United Nations, Bunche earned the Nobel Peace Prize in 1950 for his negotiations in the Arab-Israeli War. Malcolm X, from Detroit, was an insightful, powerful spokesman for African-American civil rights. "I am against every form of racism and segregation . . .," Malcolm said. "I believe in human beings, and that all human beings should be respected as such, regardless of their color."[1]

Chapter 5 ▶

History

While driving in Detroit's northern suburbs, motorists sometimes chuckle when they reach Big Beaver Road. Little do they realize that giant beavers (some up to eight feet tall, and five hundred pounds) roamed the land in Michigan thousands of years ago. So, too, did woolly mammoths and mastodons. Human beings first walked Michigan's land several thousand years ago. By 1000 B.C., people in the Upper Peninsula had created tools to mine copper. Archaeologists believe these people were the first metalworkers in North America.

The Fight for Land

In 1874, archaeologists discovered seventeen enormous mounds in southwest Michigan. More than two thousand years ago, an American Indian tribe called Hopewell built mounds as wide as a hundred feet, probably as burial sites. By the time Europeans arrived in Michigan in the 1600s, thousands of American Indians lived there. The Chippewa and Menominee inhabited the Upper Peninsula. The Ottawa, Potawatomi, Miami, and Huron tribes lived in the Lower Peninsula. These American Indians farmed the fertile land. They could fish and travel in their canoes on the many lakes, rivers, and streams.

The French were the first Europeans to discover Michigan's wonders. Explorer Étienne Brûlé, commissioned to travel from New France (Canada) to the Far East, arrived in the eastern Upper Peninsula in 1618. Early

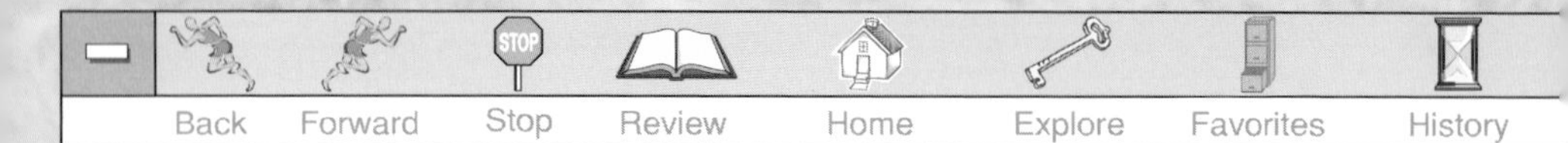

The AuSable River is beautiful in autumn. Michigan's rivers and forests have provided many natural resources for American Indians, and places for tourists to visit.

French explorers hunted fur-bearing mammals, then sold their pelts to fashion-conscious Europeans. The French also traded goods such as tools and cloth to American Indians to do the hunting and trapping for them.

As trading became big business, the French increased their presence in the territory. Father Jacques Marquette, a Jesuit missionary, established a settlement in Sault Ste. Marie in 1668. The first military outpost, Fort Michilimackinac, was built on the Straits of Mackinac in the 1670s. René Robert Cavelier, Sieur de La Salle, built the *Griffon*, the first ship to sail on the Great Lakes. In 1701, Antoine de la Mothe, Sieur de Cadillac, founded Fort Pontchartrain, a trading post that evolved into the city of Detroit.

The British, who colonized America's East Coast, coveted Michigan's resources. They entered Michigan's trading business, angering the French and many American Indians. From 1754 to 1763, the British fought the French for control of Michigan and other territory in North America. The British won, but the American Indians were not about to give up their land without a fight. In 1763, members of the Ojibwe, Potawatomi, and Ottawa tribes attacked three major British forts. Pontiac, an Ottawa chief, was one of the main figures of the rebellion. His men kept the British fort in Detroit under siege for more than 130 days before the British regained control.

Though the British defeated the French and American Indians, a new foe emerged during the American Revolution (1775–83). Despite losing the Revolutionary War, the British refused to leave their forts in Michigan. The United States gained control of the territory in 1796, then conceded major forts in Detroit and on Mackinac Island to Britain during the War of 1812. By 1815,

however, the United States had ousted the British from Michigan—this time for good.

Michigan Grows Up

Formerly a section of the Northwest Territory, Michigan became part of Indiana Territory in 1803. In 1805, the area was declared Michigan Territory. Detroit was devastated by a fire in 1805 and war during the early 1810s. A new era began in 1825 with the opening of the Erie Canal. The canal allowed Northeasterners to sail up New York's Hudson River and cross Lake Erie—right into Michigan.

Lured by stories of Michigan's fertile land, thousands of New Englanders, New Yorkers, and Pennsylvanians moved to the exciting new territory. Said one farmer in 1825, "The interior of Michigan is delightful—a mixture of prairies, oak openings and woodland, abounding in clear streams, fine lakes and cold springs."[1] The canal helped Michigan import goods while exporting lumber, ore, and food to the East. Due to "Michigan Fever," the territory's population ballooned from nine thousand people in 1820 to more than 200,000 in 1840.

Michigan applied for statehood in 1835, but two hurdles stood in its way—a controversy over the Toledo Strip, and slavery. Michigan conceded Toledo to Ohio. As compensation, the federal government gave Michigan a western section of the Upper Peninsula. As part of a compromise between the North and South, the Union accepted Michigan as a "free" state and Arkansas as a slave state. In January 1837, Michigan became the twenty-sixth state in the Union.

The exchange of Toledo for the U.P. turned out to be good for Michigan. The Upper Peninsula brimmed with iron ore and timber, and in 1841 Douglass Houghton was the first westerner to find copper in the U.P.

This scenic waterfall is indicative of the state's natural beauty and rich resources. The population of Michigan boomed between 1820 and 1840 as people from the Eastern United States looked to settle open lands.

These resources are used in the construction of ships, homes, light bulbs, and numerous other products.

As citizens of a "free" state, most Michiganders strongly opposed slavery in the South. Many worked in the Underground Railroad to provide refuge for slaves who fled north. During the Civil War (1861–65), about ninety thousand Michigan men fought in the Union Army. General George Custer, from Monroe, led the Michigan Cavalry Brigade. They contributed to the Union's victory over the Confederates in the famous Battle of Gettysburg.

A Growing Economy

After the war, the need for lumber in the Midwest grew greatly. That is because many Easterners and European immigrants moved to the area. Also, thousands of homes had to be built in Chicago after the city was destroyed by fire in 1871. To construct needed housing in the Midwest, Michigan loggers leveled millions of trees. By 1900 they had cut more than 200 billion board feet of pine logs and hardwood! At that time, more than two million people lived in Michigan. Some worked in factories, where they produced such goods as stoves, furniture, and shoes.

In the 1890s, two Michigan men worked separately on a new invention—the automobile. In Lansing, Ransom E. Olds mounted an internal combustion engine on wheels. On June 4, 1896, Henry Ford of Detroit first motored down the street in his gas-powered Quadricycle. Ford founded the Ford Motor Company to mass-produce his automobile in 1903. Only the rich could afford the new invention, until Ford introduced a no-frills Model T in 1908, and he perfected an assembly-line process that made car construction more efficient. By 1915, Ford had sold a million Model Ts.

Other Detroit automakers joined the industry. Olds merged with several others to form General Motors in 1908. Walter Chrysler founded the Chrysler Corporation in 1925. Car and auto parts plants were built in Lansing, Flint, Pontiac, and other cities. During World War I, auto factories produced tanks, trucks, and airplane engines for the United States military. Michigan literally put the "roar" into the Roaring '20s. Car making became a highly lucrative business until 1929.

In October of that year, the stock market "crashed," devastating the nation's economy. Detroit was hit especially hard since few people could afford to buy cars. Those who remained in the factories worked long hours in unsafe conditions—on slippery floors and with dangerous machines. In 1935, they formed the United Auto Workers (UAW). A year later, UAW leader Walter

In 1956, when Americans were looking to "trade up" to a mid-size vehicle, Ford began losing customers to other competitors. To combat this problem, Ford introduced the 1958 Edsel, which was also unsuccessful.

Reuther organized a sit-down strike in the General Motors plant in Flint. The strike proved successful, and autoworkers began to receive better wages and improved working conditions.

As the 1940s approached, it seemed likely that the United States would enter the escalating war in Europe. Again, Michigan's auto plants converted into war factories. Thousands of out-of-staters migrated to Detroit, including many African Americans from the South. The factories produced guns, torpedoes, even B-52 bombers. One Chrysler plant churned out 25,000 tanks. Detroit became known nationwide as the "Arsenal of Democracy." After the United States joined the war in December 1941, 600,000 Michiganders served. About fifteen thousand never returned.

Michigan in the Modern Era

Though war production ended in 1945, America's economy boomed after the war. Millions of Americans wanted new cars—and that meant jobs and money for Michigan. By the mid-1950s, Detroit was producing nine million cars a year. Many cars, some like the 1957 Chevy, were big and sleek with shiny chrome and fancy fins.

Cars changed Americans' way of life, including the people from Michigan. Detroiters moved to the suburbs and commuted to work. Highways were constructed, and in 1957 the Mackinac Bridge opened. It took three years to construct "Mighty Mac," but for the first time people could drive from the Lower Peninsula to the Upper Peninsula.

Detroit's golden era dimmed in the 1960s. Consumer advocate Ralph Nader exposed safety problems with American cars. People started buying more cars from other countries. Racial tensions simmered in Detroit.

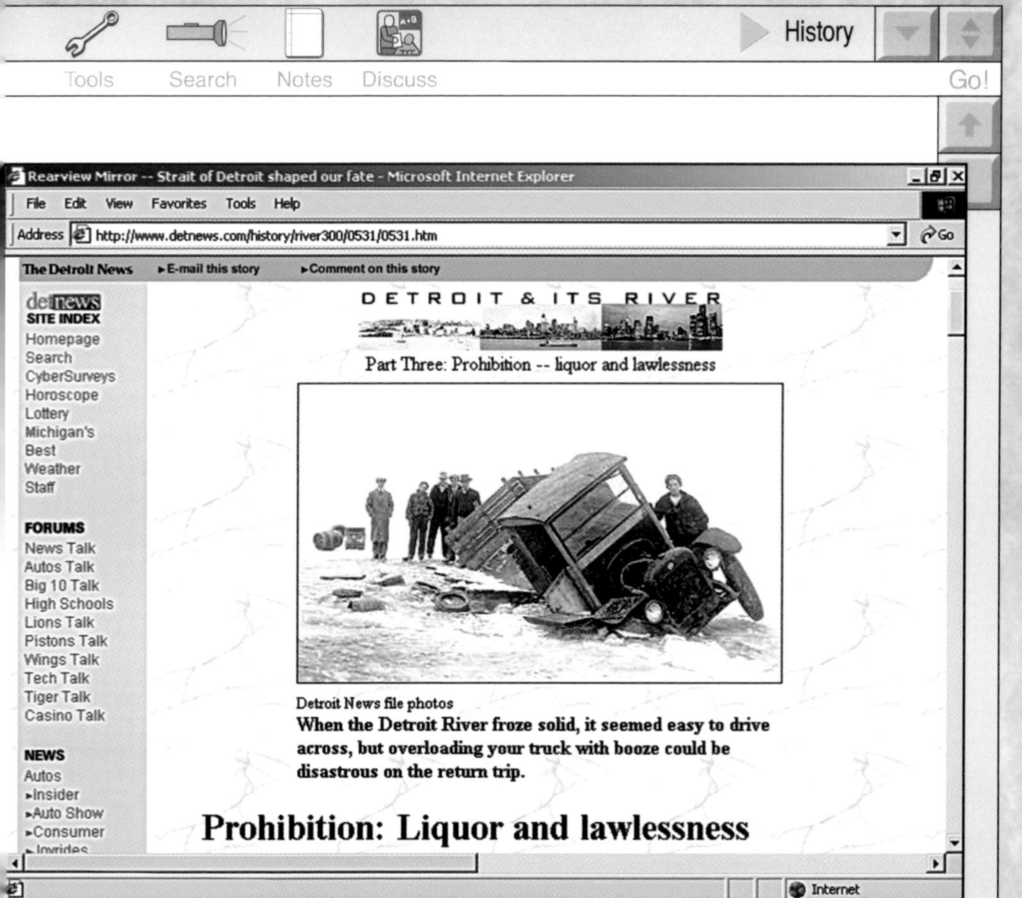

In the 1920s, during Prohibition, Canada allowed people to distill liquor. People smuggled liquor across the Detroit River heading to countries such as Cuba or Venezuela where it was legal to drink.

African Americans faced discrimination, as they were turned down for jobs, loans, and housing. Most were crowded into low-income areas, where they endured harsh treatment by police. In July 1967, such harassment triggered a three-day riot. Stores were burned, guns fired, and 43 people were killed—mostly African Americans.

In 1968, the Michigan Fair Housing Law made it illegal to discriminate in the sale or rental of housing. Coleman Young, elected mayor in 1973, created many job opportunities for African Americans in city government.

The Detroit skyline can be quite an amazing sight. The city itself saw improvement in the living conditions of its residents toward the end of the twentieth century.

Still, living conditions in Detroit continued to decline, while crime and unemployment rates rose.

Attempts to revitalize Detroit's downtown area—for example, the construction of the Renaissance Center—failed. Those who could afford to move to the suburbs did so. The population of Detroit, which had approached two million during the 1950s, dropped to six digits. Eventually, thanks to Michigan's prosperity in the 1990s, living conditions in Detroit improved. From 1990 to 2000, the number of Detroiters living in poverty dropped

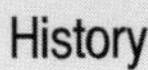
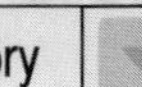

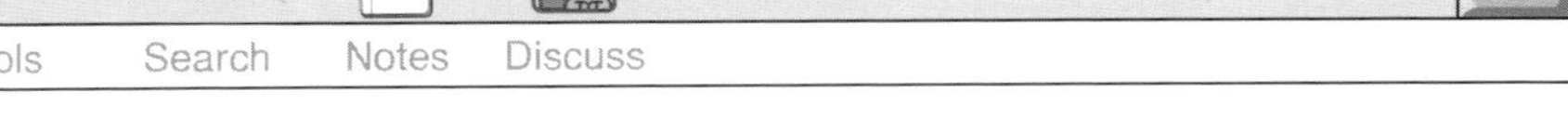

from 32 percent (the highest in the nation) to 20 percent (sixteenth in the nation).

Over the 1980s and 1990s, suburbanites have moved farther and farther west and north. In fact, some "suburban Detroiters" now live closer to Ann Arbor and Flint than to Detroit itself. They enjoy the open land on the far outskirts of Detroit—hills, lakes, woods, and fresh air. It is often a long commute to work and to visit relatives. For Michiganders, that is acceptable to them. After all, they love to drive.

Chapter Notes

Chapter 1. The Great Lakes State

1. H. A. Musham, "Early Great Lakes Steamboats," *The American Neptune,* XVIII, No. 4:293.

2. Tom Yates, "Motown Historical Museum—Golden Memories," *Detroit Metropolitan Airport News,* n.d., <http://www.dtwnews.com/tom/motown_historical_museum.htm> (November 28, 2002).

Chapter 3. Economy

1. Bruce Catton, *Michigan: A Bicentennial History* (New York: W. W. Norton & Company, Inc., 1976), p. 191.

2. Melinda Clynes, "Eastern Market," *Metro Times Detroit,* n.d., <http://www.metrotimes.com/19/AVG99B/Features/AVGb-Junk.htm.> (December 8, 2002).

Chapter 4. Government

1. Malcolm X, *By Any Means Necessary* (New York: Pathfinder Press, 1970), p. 158.

Chapter 5. History

1. Ronald Shaw, "Michigan Influences upon the Formative Years of the Erie Canal," *Michigan History,* XXXVII, No. 1, pp. 7, 10.

Further Reading

Anderson, Erin. *Look About You: A Magical Childhood in Michigan's Wild Places.* Cedar, Mich.: Rimwalk Press, 2002.

Capstone Press Staff. *Michigan.* Minnetonka, Minn.: Capstone Press, Incorporated, 2003.

Carney, Tom. *Natural Wonders of Michigan: Exploring Wild and Scenic Places.* New York: McGraw-Hill/Contemporary Books, 1999.

Dunbar, Willis F. *Michigan: A History of the Wolverine State.* Grand Rapids: Eerdmans Publishing Company, 1995.

Gavrilovich, Peter and Bill McGraw, eds. *The Detroit Almanac.* Detroit: Detroit Free Press, 2000.

Gay, Cheri Y. *Detroit, Then & Now.* San Diego: Thunder Bay Press, 2001.

Hintz, Martin. *Michigan.* Danbury, Conn.: Children's Press, 1998.

Rubenstein, Bruce A. and Lawrence E. Ziewacz. *Michigan: A History of the Great Lakes State.* Wheeling, Ill.: Harlan Davidson, 2002.

Thompson, Kathleen. *Michigan.* Austin, Tex.: Raintree Steck-Vaughn Publishers, 1996.

Wargin, Kathy-Jo. *Michigan: The Spirit of the Land.* Stillwater, Minn.: Voyageur Press, 1999.

———. *The Michigan Reader: For Boys and Girls.* Chelsea, Mich.: Sleeping Bear Press, 2001.

Index